INNER PAGES' ILLUSTRATED CLASSICS

ANTOINE DE SAINT-EXUPÉRY'S

The Little Prince

Retold by W. Sequeira & A. D' Souza and Re-illustrated.

INNER PAGES

THE LITTLE PRINCE

ISBN 81-7929-224-X

First Edition of 18 Titles 2001, Reprinted 2002, 2003, 2004 (Twice), 2005 (For export), 2006, 2007, 2008. This title added to the series in 2010
Reprinted 2011, 2012

Published for:
ADARSH ENTERPRISES
4393/4 Tulsidas Street, Ansari Road,
Darya Ganj, New Delhi-110002
Phones: 23246131, 23246132. Fax: 011-23246130.
Email: adarshbooks@vsnl.com

Printed at : Thakur Enterprises, Delhi

Contents

Contents

LIVING WITH GROWNUPS

At the age of six, I recall, possessing a book called True Stories from Nature about the Primeval Forest. This book had beautiful pictures; the one that I remember showed a boa constrictor attempting to swallow an animal. The picture looked quite like the one below.

The book explained that the Boa constrictors swallowed their prey without

A Boa Constrictor swallowing an animal

chewing them. Having swallowed them, they became fat and were unable to move so they slept for as long as six months, to digest what they had eaten.

Browsing through the book I had thoughts about adventures in the jungle. In an attempt to put my thoughts on paper, I took a pencil and drew my first picture. My first drawing looked something like the picture on the adjoining page.

To impress a few grown-ups and to get a their opinion, I showed them my picture and asked them if they were frightened by it.

On seeing the picture they answered: 'Frightened? How can that frighten anyone? It is just a hat'

They got it all wrong. It was not a picture of a hat. Since they were not able to understand the picture and knowing well

My first drawings

that grown-ups had to be explained everything, I decided to make another picture for their sake.

In my new drawing I drew the elephant, inside the boa constrictor's stomach so that they could understand my drawing. My new picture looked like the one below the last picture.

To my surprise the grown-ups' advised me to set aside my drawings of a Boa constrictor's anatomy and concentrate on the subjects like Grammar, History, Geography and Arithmetic being taught in school. This is the point when I ended my career as a painter disheartened and disillusioned with the poor response to my two drawings. I wonder why grown-ups don't understand anything and why do children have to explain everything to them.

It was after this that I decided to choose another profession. I now decided to become a pilot. The geography that I learnt in school has been very useful to me and I have now flown all over the world. In fact my geography is so good that at a glass I can distinguish between China and as Arizona. Beyond doubt such knowledge is valuable in case one gets lost at night.

Also my life I have been in touch with all kinds of people. I have actually lived a great deal with grown-ups. While living with them and had a chance of studying them closely however this is not chain my opinion in any way.

On occasions I felt that I met a grown-up who seemed sensible and clear-sighted. Not wanting to miss the opportunity I showed the grown-up my first drawing just to test the grown-up's understanding. Sadly so the answer was always:

'That looks like a hat.'

Having heard the response I would never talk to that grown-up about boa constrictors, primeval forests or stars. Instead I would bring myself down to discussing golf, politics, and bridge. The grown-up would of course be elated because he had met such a sensible person (me).

THE FIRST MEETING

It was under these circumstances that I lived my life alone and never, really, had anyone I could talk to. I never expected things to change but life had something else in store for me.

Six years ago, the plane I was flying, developed a problem in the engine, while flying over the Sahara. I landed and checked the engine. Stranded in the Sahara, I decided to carry out the repairs myself because, I had food and water which would not last me more than seven days.

Tired after the harrowing experience and thousands of miles from the nearest habitation, I spent my first night in the desert and slept on the sand. My plight was no different from a shipwrecked sailor floating away on driftwood in the middle of the ocean.

My amazement knew no bounds when I was awaked in the morning by a child's voice, which said:

'Please! Can you draw me a sheep?'

'What!' I said.

'Can you draw me a sheep?'

Completely bewildered I rose to my feet, rubbed my eyes and looked around. Standing next to me was a small boy with as serious

A sketch of that small boy

look on his face. I have drawn below, from my memory much later, a sketch of what he looked like. It would not be wrong to say that the little boy looked much better than what you see in the picture.

The poor picture is not really my fault. Remember my career as a painter ended at the age of six when I drew boa constrictors with elephants inside them.

Getting back to the reality of having crashed in the Sahara desert, thousands of miles from habitation, I stared with astonishment at the little boy. In the middle of the desert the boy did not seem to be fainting from thirst or hunger, nor was there a trace of fear or fatigue on his face.

At last I managed to speak to him and I said to him:

'But what is it that you are doing here?'

The reply was soft and slow, as if to emphasise an important matter at hand:

'If you please could you draw me a sheep'.

There are occasions when you are at a loss of words, and for me this was one. Thousands of miles from any habitation, in danger of death from thirst and hunger I was too astonished to say anything. I obeyed and pulled out a piece of paper and a pen from my pocket. However recalling how studying Grammar, History, Geography and Arithmetic in school had cut short my career as a painter, I told the little boy (a little sternly) that I did not know how to draw.

On hearing this, the little boy answered:

'It really doesn't matter. Please draw me a sheep'

The problem was I had never drawn a sheep before. Seeing the boy's persistence, I

The sheep and the box

drew him a picture of the boa constrictor, the one that was confused for a hat by the grown-ups, and handed it over to the little boy.

I was taken aback by the boy's response, on seeing the picture I had given him.

'No! no! I don't want the picture of an elephant inside a boa constrictor. Boas are dangerous and elephants are cumbersome. I want you to draw me a sheep because, where I live, everything is very small. So just draw me a sheep'.

Sensing I could not get out of it, I drew a sheep and handed the picture out to him.

The boy carefully examined the picture and said:

'This sheep looks sick. Can you draw me a better one?'

So I drew another one and gave it to him.

On seeing the picture the boy smiled gently

A picture of the Ram

and said:

'This is not a sheep, it is a Ram with horns.'

Knowing what was coming, I drew another one. This too was rejected.

'This sheep is too old. I want a sheep that will live for many years.'

My patience ended and the urgency to start repairs to my plane's engine forced me to toss the drawing aside and draw a new one as shown in the picture.

As I handed him the picture, I explained:

'This is only the box, the sheep is inside it'.

I saw surprise on the boy's face as he said:

'That is exactly how I wanted it. Do you think this sheep will eat a lot of grass?'

'Why do you ask?'

'It is because, where I live, everything is very small.'

'There would surely be enough grass for such a small sheep.'

Hearing this the boy bent his head over he drawing and examined it:

'Not so small that..... Look! He has gone to sleep.'

This was how I met the 'Little Prince'.

A HOUSE FOR THE SHEEP

It was not easy for me to find out where the Little Prince came from. He was constantly asking a lot of questions but not willing to answer any. It was only through the conversation that I had with him that I came to know where he came from.

For instance, when he first saw my aeroplane, (I will not be able to draw the plane for you since it is too complicated) he pointed out to the aeroplane and asked me:

'What is that you have there?'

'That is an aeroplane, it is my aeroplane and it is used for flying.'

I felt proud in letting him know that I could fly a plane.

On hearing this he cried out:

'What! You mean you dropped down from the sky?'

I replied modestly in the affirmative.

His surprise grew and he said:

'Oh! That is very funny!'

With this the Little Prince broke into a peal of laughter, much to my irritation. It was as if someone was laughing at my misfortune. Having laughed it off he said:

'So you too came from the sky. Which planet are you from?'

The Little Prince was lost in thought

It was at that moment that I felt he had said something that needed to be questioned, so as to solve the mystery of his presence in the middle of the desert. I asked him:

'Are you from another planet?'

As usual he did not respond to my question. He just tossed his head and continued to stare at my aeroplane.

'It is true that on that you couldn't have come from very far away.......'

Having said that he sank into a long reverie. Then, he took the picture of the sheep from his pocket and started contemplating about his treasure.

'My curiosity knew no bounds since his statement about 'the other planets'. So I attempted to find out some more about it.

'My little man, where do you come from? Where is this "Where I live" that you speak of and where do you want to take your sheep?'

In silence he reflected for some time and then replied:

'What I really like about the box you have drawn is that the sheep can use it as a house at night.'

'Is that so. If you are good then I will also give you a string to tie him with during the day and a post to tie him to.'

The Little Prince seemed offended at my offer.

'Tie him up? What a queer idea.'

'But if you do not tie him up, he will stray, wander off somewhere and then get lost.'

Once again the Little Prince broke into a peal of laughter:

'But where would he go?'

'Anywhere or just straight ahead of him.'

To this the Little Prince responded seriously:

'It really doesn't matter, Everything is so small where I live.' With a sad expression on his face he went on to add: 'Straight ahead of him, he cannot go very far.....'

REMEMBERING A FRIEND

It was during this conversation that I was able to uncover another important fact in my attempts to find out where the Little Prince came from.

I now knew that he came from a planet, which was not larger than a house.

Though it was and astounding fact, I was not really surprised about it because I knew that amongst the larger planets like Earth,

A Planet smaller than a house

Mars, Venus and Jupiter, there were many small planets which could not even be seen with the help of the best telescopes.

On occasions when an Astronomer discovers a small new planet, he does not even give it a name, he just assigns a number to it, for example he may call it 'Asteroid 325'.

Assigning such a name to a planet or asteroid, makes it easy for the grown-ups to accept its existence.

If my knowledge is correct, there exists an asteroid called B-612, it is so small that it cannot be seen with the naked eye.

I have reason to believe it is this planet wherefrom the Little Prince has come. A Turkish astronomer first observed this asteroid, in 1909, through a telescope.

After discovering the asteroid, the astronomer had made public his discovery to

The Astronomer

the International Astronomical Congress, during a conference. Unfortunately no one believed him because of his Turkish attire and origin.

This incident angered the Turkish dictator, who wanted Turkey to be recognised for the discovery. His anger prompted him to pass a law, under pain of death, asking all his subjects to change their attire and wear European clothes.

Later in 1920 the same astronomer, dressed in European attire, made the discovery public in the conference.

On this occasion everyone in the room accepted his discovery.

I had reason for memorizing the facts about Asteroid B-612 and likewise a reason for telling you about it.

It was to bring your attention to the ways

No one believed the astronomer

of the grown-ups. You see! Grown-ups like numbers. If you tell them that you have made a new friend, they would not ask you about his habits or hobbies.

In other words they would not ask you: What games does he like to play? Does he collect butterflies? Or for that matter: What does his voice sound like?

On the contrary they would ask: How old is he? How many brothers and sisters does he have? How much does he weigh? Or How much money does his father make? They attempt to learn about your friend only from the numbers you can narrate about him.

If you were to tell the grown-ups: 'I've seen a beautiful house made of red bricks, having geraniums on the windowsill and doves on the roof…' they would not be able to understand what you are saying.

The astronomer dressed in European attire

On the contrary, to make them understand, you would have to say to them: 'I saw a house that costs four thousand pounds.' It is only then that they would exclaim" 'Oh! What a pretty house it is'.

Thus if you said to them: 'I met the Little Prince, he was charming, he laughed and was looking for a sheep. The fact that someone is looking for a sheep, very much, proves that he exists,' all this would do no good and prove nothing to them.

They would just shrug their shoulders and treat you like a child. But if you told them: 'I met a Little Prince who came from the Asteroid B-612,' then they would be satisfied and not ask you any more questions.

Grown-ups are like that. Children should always show great forbearance towards them.

Those of us, who understand life, do not care that much about numbers. I would have, very much, liked to start this story like fairy tale saying: Once upon a time there was a Little Prince who lived on a planet which was not much bigger than himself and who needed a friend....'

For those who understand life, this would have been a much better way of beginning a story with an air of truth in it.

I do not want my book to be read carelessly. I have suffered much grief in penning down my memories. It has been six years since I lost my little friend and his sheep.

I write about him only to remember him because forgetting a friend can be sad. Not all of us have friends. If I forget my friend then I will be like the other grown-ups who are not interested in anything but numbers.....

With just that intention in mind, I bought some paints and pencils. I knew it was not easy to start painting at my age, especially since I had not made any pictures in my life, except at the age of six when I drew the inside of a boa constrictor.

Even though I am not sure about it, I will try to make my portraits as true to life as possible. One drawing may come out well but the next one may not show the subject properly or bear resemblance to the subject.

There are other errors as well, in some pictures the height of the Little Prince is not right. In some pictures he is too tall, while in others he is too short.

I have my doubts about the colour of his costume as well. Still I fumble along, good in some places and bad in others, hoping to get a generally acceptable result.

There are other details in which I have made mistakes as well. But that is something, which is not my fault, and I will have to be forgiven for it. Unfortunately my friend never explained anything to me.

Perhaps, he thought I was quite like him. Alas, I do not know how to see sheep inside closed boxes. Come to think of it, perhaps like the grown-ups, I too have to grow old.

TENDING TO THE BAOBABS

As time passed and as I talked to the Little Prince, I would learn something new, about his departure from his planet and his journey from thereon. The information came in bits and pieces following the course of the Little Prince's thoughts. It was only on the third day that I came to know about the baobabs catastrophe.

Once again I had the sheep to thank for it. On

one occasion, with a look of doubt on his face, the Little Prince asked me: 'Is it true or not that sheep eat little bushes?'

'Yes! That is true.' I replied.

'Ah! I am glad.' He said.

I could not understand why it was important, for the Little Prince, that sheep should eat little bushes. But then he added:

'Then it can be concluded that they also eat baobabs?'

Since baobabs are trees which are as tall as castles and not even a herd of elephants would be able to eat a single baobab, I pointed out to the Little Prince that baobabs were not small bushes and even if he took a herd of elephants, they would not be able to eat a baobab.

On hearing of the elephants the Little Prince laughed at the idea and said:

'We would have to stack them up one on top of the other.' But then he commented wisely:

A stack of elephants

'Before they grow into big trees, baobabs start out by being little.'

Continuing the conversation I agreed:

'That is so very true, but why would your sheep want to eat the small baobabs?'

He responded at once: 'Oh! Come, come!' quite as if he was talking of something that was quite evident. And I was forced to make a mental effort to resolve this problem without any help.

I learned that, quite like on all planets, there were on the Little Prince's planet good plants and bad plants. As consequence of this, the good plants produced good seeds, while the bad plants produced bad seeds. However the seeds were invisible.

Until they suddenly decide to wake up, the seeds sleep deep in the heart of the earth's darkness. When it decides to wake up, a little seed stretches itself, and timidly in the beginning, pushes a tiny sprig inoffensively upwards towards the sun. If it is the sprout of a rose bush or a radish, one must let it grow where it wishes to. But if it is the sprig of a bad plant, like a weed, one must destroy it by rooting it out, as soon as it is recognised as a bad plant.

On the Little Prince's planet the seeds of the baobab was considered bad since the soil of the planet was infested with them. If it was not uprooted in time it would spread and you would never get rid of the baobab and it would spread all over the planet and the strong roots would bore right through the planet. Since the planet was very small, too many baobabs would split the planet into pieces.....

Later on the Little Prince said to me: 'It is a question of discipline, when you have finished your toilet in the morning, you attend to it.'

Uprooting the small Baobabs

'Just so, you must attend to the planet's toilet with similar care. You must pull out the baobabs, very regularly, the moment you are able to distinguish them from the rose bushes they resemble in the early days of their growth. The work is tedious but is also very easy.' Added the Little Prince.

One day the Little Prince said to me: 'You ought to make a beautiful picture so that the children, where you live, can see what this is like. It would be very helpful to them if they were to travel some day. You may like to put aside some work for another day but in the case of the baobabs, it would be a disaster to do so. I know of a planet where there was a lazy man who neglected three little bushes....'

Based on the Little Prince's description, I made a picture of the planet. Though I do not wish to act like a moralist, but everyone does

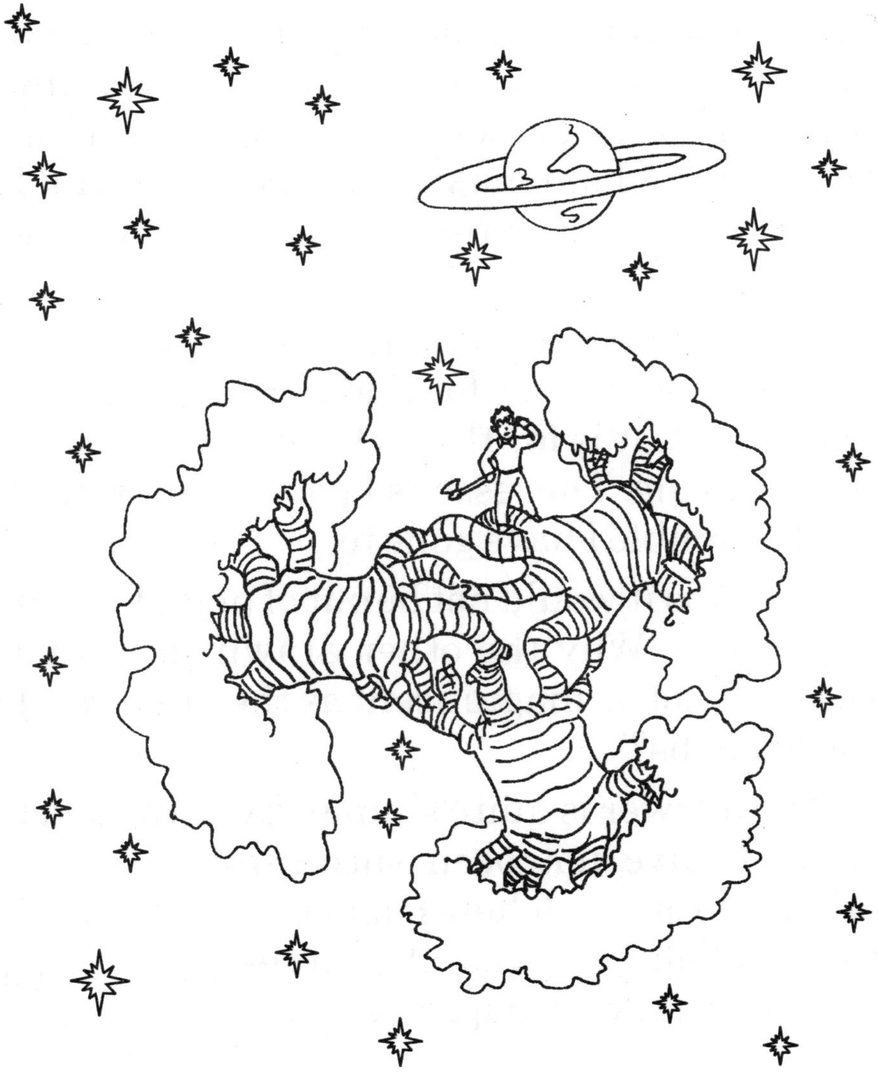

The planet with the neglected Baobabs

not understand the danger of the baobabs and the risks are considerable to someone who might get lost on an asteroid. Keeping this in mind I am making an exception and I say plainly: 'Children, watch out for the baobabs!'

Quite like me, my friends have been skirting the danger for a long time, without knowing it. It is for them that I have created this drawing. The lessons I pass on are worth all the trouble I have gone to.

Perhaps it would not be out of place for you to ask me: 'Why the other drawings in this book are not as magnificent as the drawing of the baobabs?'

The answer is quite simple: Even though I tried, I have not been successful with the others because, when I made a drawing of the baobabs, it was the necessity of the purpose that was inspiring me.

WATCHING SUNSETS

'Oh. Little Prince! It is only bit-by-bit that I have come to understand the secrets of your life.... For a very long time you were entertained by quietly watching the setting sun.' It was only on the fourth day that I learned a new detail when you said to me:

'I' am very fond of sunsets. Come let us go now and watch the setting sun.'

'But we must wait,' I said.

Watching the sun set

'Wait? Why?' the Little Prince responded.

'We must wait till it is time for the sun to set.'

At first he seemed surprised, he then laughed to himself and said:

'I always keep thinking I am at home!'

Quite everyone knows that, when it is noon in the United States, the sun is setting over France. What would it be like if you could, within one minute, fly over to France? You could fly straight from the noon into the sunset. France, unfortunately, is too far away for that. On your tiny planet, it is different. All you need to do is, to move your chair a few steps and you could see the day ending and the twilight falling wherever you want.

'One day,' you had told me 'I had watched the sun set forty-four times' and some time later you added:

'You know.... when one is sad, one loves the sunset...'

'On the day you watched the forty-four sunsets, were you so sad?' I asked.

The Little Prince did not reply.

MATTERS OF GREAT CONSEQUENCE

On the fifth day another secret of the Little Prince's life was revealed to me, once again thanks to the sheep. Very abruptly and without anything leading to it, and quite out of silent contemplation the Little Prince questioned me about a problem, which, seemingly, had been on his mind for quite some time. He asked:

'If a sheep eats bushes, does it eat flowers as well?'

'A sheep would eat anything edible that it can find with its reach.' I said.

'It would even eat flowers that have thorns?'

'Yes! It would eat even flowers that have thorns on them.' I replied.

My thoughts were elsewhere. I was busy trying to unscrew a bolt that was stuck in the engine of my plane. It had me worried because I was beginning to realize that the breakdown in my plane was very serious. I had very little drinking water left and I feared the worst might happen and I may die of thirst.

'What use are the thorns?' the Little Prince asked.

I knew that the Little Prince never let go

of the question once he had asked it. All my attention was towards the bolt and just to get it over with, I answered with whatever came to my head:

'The thorns are useless. Flowers have thorns just for the sake of it!'

'Oh!' exclaimed the Little Prince.

With that there was complete silence for a moment. And then, quite restlessly, he responded to me:

'I cannot believe you! Flowers are weak and naïve and they need to reassure themselves. They believe that the thorns are terrible weapons...'

I did not respond to him and said to myself:

'I am going to knock this bolt with a hammer if it fails to turn.' The Little Prince, once again, broke into my thoughts:

'Do you actually believe that flowers have...'

'Oh, no!' I cried. 'No, no, no! I don't believe anything. I just responded to you with whatever came to my mind. Can't you see I am busy with a matter of consequence!'

The Little Prince was thunderstruck.

'Matter of consequence!' he retorted.

He continued to stare at my fingers, covered with engine grease and holding a hammer, and bending over an object that looked extremely ugly....

'You spoke just like the grown-ups'

I felt a little ashamed. However he went on relentlessly:

'You mix everything up... you confuse everything...'

The Little Prince was really angry and he tossed his curls in the air.

'I know of a planet where there is a red-faced gentleman who has never smelled a flower or looked at a star. He has never loved anybody. All he has done in his life is add up numbers. Very much like you, he keeps repeating all day that he is engrossed in matters of great consequence. Though it makes him swell up in pride, I know that he is not a man, he is a mushroom.' Said the Little Prince.

'A what?' I asked.

'A mushroom!' replied the Little Prince, now white with rage.

'Flowers and thorns have been growing for millions of years. Similarly sheep have been eating all the while. I don't see why it is a matter of consequence to try to understand why flowers grow thorns when they are useless for them. Is the war between the

Flowers and thorns

sheep and the flowers not important? Is it not more important than the sums of a red-faced gentleman? If I know of one flower that is unique and grows nowhere except on my planet, and one fine morning a little sheep destroys it in a single bite, without even knowing what he is doing. Don't you think that is more important?'

With a blush on his face the Little Prince continued:

'If you love a flower which is one of a kind on the millions and millions of stars around you, it should be enough to make you happy whenever you look at the stars because you can say to yourself:'

'The flower I love is somewhere out there... But if a sheep eats the flower then, for him, it is as if all the stars had stopped twinkling! Don't you feel that is important!'

With tears in his eyes the Little Prince became silent. By then the sun had set and night had fallen. Without caring about my hammer, my bolt or my thirst, I dropped my tools simply because there was on my planet earth a Little Prince who needed to be comforted. It was with this feeling that I took him into my arms and said:

'The flower that you are so fond of is not in danger. I will draw you a railing that you can put round the flower and a muzzle that you can for your sheep. I will...'

I was at a loss of words and did not know what to say to him. I felt awkward. I did not know how to console him or how to go hand in hand with him once again.

The land of tears is truly a secret place.

THE FLOWER

Soon I began to understand the flowers on the Little Prince's planet. They were very simple because they had only one ring of petals; they took up no space and they troubled no one.

In the mornings they would appear on the grass and in the evening they would fade away in peace. Things change, when one day a seed carried from somewhere, by the wind landed on the Little Prince's planet and in no time a new flower bloomed. Like always the Little Prince had watched the sprouting because it could have been a new kind of baobab that might have to be rooted out.

This one was different because soon it stopped growing and began to produce a flower.

The Little Prince was present when the first bud appeared. The bud was huge and it seemed as if a strange apparition would appear from it.

The flower prepared for blooming very slowly, it chose its colours with care, well shielded in its green sheath.

It adjusted its petals gradually, as if attempting to appear in the world in a dignified manner and in full radiance quite different from a field of poppies. This went on

A new flower had bloomed

for quite a few days.

Finally, one fine morning, exactly as the sun rose, she unveiled herself with painstaking precision. With a yawn she said:

'Ah! I am barely awake. I beg to be excused since some of my petals are disarranged...'

Seeing this the Little Prince could not hold back his admiration and awe. He said:

'Oh! You are very beautiful.'

Very sweetly the flower responded:

'No! I am not, I was born with the first rays of the sun.'

The Little Prince could see that she was being modest because she was truly beautiful.

The flower spoke once again:

'I think I need some breakfast. Would you be kind enough to...'

Breakfast for the flower

Hearing this the Little Prince went searching for a sprinkling can and water so that he could tend to the flower.

Soon she began to bother him with her vanity and that was a little difficult for the Little Prince to deal with.

On one occasion, she began talking about her four thorns and said:

'Let the tigers come with their claws!'

'But there are no tigers on my planet.' Responded the Little Prince.

'Anyway, tigers do not eat weeds.'

Hearing this she responded:

'I am not a weed.'

'Please excuse me...' said the Little Prince.

'I am not afraid of tigers,' she continued, 'but I am horrified by draughts. Would you

Tigers never ate weeds

have a screen for me?'

'Draughts are bad luck for a plant,' remarked the Little Prince to the flower. Then added to himself 'This flower is quite a complex creature...'

The flower continued, 'Cover me with a glass globe at night; it is very cold on your planet. Where I come from....'

At this point the flower feel silent, she realized that she had come to this planet in the form of a seed, which was carried by the wind and she had no way of knowing what it was like in other places.

Feeling embarrassed over the slip of her tongue and at being caught on the verge of such an untruth, she pretended to cough as if something was caught in her throat.

'The screen! Where is the screen?' she said instead.

Protecting the flower from the cold

'I was going to look for it and get it when you spoke to me...' said the Little Prince.

The flower coughed once more, probably to build a feeling of remorse in the Little Prince. Though the Little Prince fell inseparable from the flower, he had begun to doubt her.

He had understood the words of the flower, they were of no importance but it made him unhappy all the same.

'I should not have listened to the flower,' he told me one day. 'One should never listen to flowers; one should simply admire and smell them.

My flower spread its fragrance all over my planet. This tale disturbed me very much though it should have only filled my heart with tenderness and pity.'

The Little Prince continued to share his inner most thoughts:

'Since I did not know how to understand anything! I should have judged, not by the words but by the deeds. She had cast her fragrance and radiance over me and I should not have run away from her... I should have understood all the affection that was within her. Flowers have no consistency and I was too young to understand how to love her...'

LEAVING THE PLANET

I suspect he escaped from his planet by taking advantage of migrating wild birds. On the morning of his departure he put everything in perfect order on his planet. He possessed two active volcanoes, which he used for heating his breakfast every morning. Before leaving he swept them both. 'He also had an extinct volcano about which he said, 'You never know!' So he swept the extinct volcano as well. As he said, if you kept the volcanoes clean then they did not erupt, instead they burn gradually and gently. Here on Earth we cannot keep our volcanoes clean because we are very small that is why they erupt and cause so much damage.

With a sense of sorrow, since he was leaving, the Little Prince tore up the remaining baobab shoots. Though he knew he would never return, he did all this because he had a sense of responsibility, on the last morning he would spend on his planet. He felt like crying, when he watered his flower for the last time and lifted the glass dome to place it over the flower

Looking at the flower he said, 'Goodbye.'

The flower did not respond.

'Goodbye,' he said once again.

The flower coughed and whispered, 'I have

Sweeping the volcanoes

been silly so please forgive me. Try to be happy.'

The absence of reproaches surprised him and he stood for a moment, with the glass globe in his hand, failing to understand that quiet sweetness.

The flower said:

'Of course I love you and it is my fault if you did not sense it. It is not important, but you have also been as foolish as me. Leave the glass dome; I don't need it any longer. Just try to be happy....'

'But what about the wind...' said the Little Prince?

'My cold is not that bad.... I am a flower and the cool night air will do me some good.'

'Then what about the animals....'

'I will have to tolerate a few caterpillars if I want to see a few butterflies. I know they are very beautiful. If not the butterflies, who will call upon me when you are far away? And I am not afraid of the large animals, I too have claws.' With this she showed me her four thorns. She continued: 'don't irritate me by hanging around, since you have decided to leave then you should go.

She said it all because she didn't want him to see her crying. A proud flower she was....

MEETING A KING

Having left his planet, he soon found himself in the vicinity of asteroids 325, 326, 327, 328, 329 and 330. With an intention of adding to his knowledge, he decided to visit them.

A king inhabited the first asteroid he visited. The king was dressed in purple and ermine and was seated on a simple but majestic throne.

The King of the first asteroid

On seeing the Little Prince the king exclaimed:

'Ah! Here comes a subject.'

Hearing this the Little Prince said to himself:

'How can he recognize me when he has never seen me before' little did the prince know it is very simple for Kings? For them everyone is a subject.

'Approach me so that I can see you properly.' Said the king feeling rather proud that he finally had a subject and was a king to someone.

The little Prince looked around for a place to sit, he found none because almost the entire planet was covered by the king's ermine robe. Not finding a place to sit, the Little Prince continued to stand. Tired after his journey, the Little Prince could not hold back a yawn.

On seeing the Little Prince yawn the king said:

'I forbid you to yawn, it is bad manners to yawn in the presence of a king.'

With an embarrassed look on his face, the Little Prince responded:

'I cannot help it, I have come here after a long journey, without any sleep, and I am tired.'

'Oh! If that is so,' said the king, 'then I order you to yawn, it has been a long time since I have seen somebody yawning. I find yawns curious. So I order you to yawn once again.'

The Little Prince blushed and said, 'you frighten me... I cannot yawn anymore...'

'Hum! Hum!' responded the king. 'Then...I...I order yawn sometimes and sometimes...'

The king spluttered and seemed vexed.

What the king really wanted was that his authority be respected. He would tolerate no disobedience since he was an absolute monarch. He was also kind hearted, which is why his orders were reasonable.

Very timidly the Little Prince asked:

'May I sit down?'

'Yes! I order you to do so,' the king answered immediately and quite majestically gathered a fold of his ermine robe.

The Little Prince wondered what the king ruled over, the planet was extremely tiny.

Out of curiosity the Little Prince asked:

'Sire…' he said 'Please excuse me but may I ask you a question.'

'I order you to ask me a question' the king responded.

'Sire... what is it that you rule over?'

'I rule over everything,' the king replied.

'Over everything?' asked the Little Prince.

The king made a sweeping gesture, which included his own planet and all the planets and stars in the sky.

'You rule over all that?' asked the Little Prince in surprise.

'Yes! Over all that,' answered the king.

The king considered his rule to be absolute and universal.

'Even the stars obey you?'

'They certainly do,' said the king. 'They obey me instantaneously I don't tolerate insubordination.'

The Little Prince was impressed by such power. If the king had so much authority then he would watching the sunset, not forty-four times a day, but seventy two times or even a hundred times a day, that too without moving his chair. Since he felt a little sad at having let his planet, he plucked up some courage and asked the king for a favour:

'I would like to see the sun set.... Please be kind enough to order the sun to set.'

'If I was to order a military general to fly like a butterfly from one flower to another, or if I was to ask him to write a tragic drama, or, for that matter, to change himself into a sea bird, and if the general did not obey my order then who do you think would be at fault?' the king asked. 'The general or myself?'

'You would be at fault,' said the Little Prince firmly.

'Precisely,' the King responded. 'I have the right to demand from anyone, what he or she is capable of. Authority is always based on reason. You will only end up with a revolution if you ask your people to throw themselves into the sea. I have the right to demand obedience only if my orders are reasonable and can be followed.'

'But what about my sunset?' the Little Prince reminded him, as usual not forgetting a question once he had asked it.

'I will demand a sunset and you shall have it, but it will be based on the scientific principles of governance. I will wait till the conditions are favourable,' replied the King.

'And when will that happen?' asked the Little Prince.

The King hummed, rubbed his nose and consulted a big calendar and responded, 'It will happen around twenty minutes to eight, this evening. It is then that you will see that I am obeyed.'

Regretting his lost sunset, the Little Prince yawned with boredom and said, 'I have nothing else to do here so I shall be on my way.'

'Don't leave just yet,' said the king feeling proud on finally having a subject, 'I will make you a minister on my planet!'

'You will make me a minister of what?' queried the Little Prince.

'A minister of ... Justice!' replied the king.

'But you have no one, on your planet, to judge!'

'We cannot be sure of that yet,' said the king. 'I still haven't toured my kingdom. I am old, walking makes me feel tired and I have no room for a horse and carriage on my planet.'

'Oh! But I have already looked around,' said the Little Prince, glancing around the planet a second time, just to be sure.

'If that be so, you will judge yourself,' responded the king. 'It is by far the most difficult thing to do. If you can judge yourself well then you are wise, else you are a fool.'

'If I have to judge myself, then I can do it anywhere. I don't have to live here to judge myself.' Said the Little Prince.

'Hum! Hum!' said the king. 'I think there is an old rat living on my planet, I have often heard him moving around at night, you can judge him.' Said the king. 'You can condemn him to death time and again, and then spare his life to keep him alive. This way his life will depend on your justice. You see! He is the only rat we have on the planet.'

'I think I will be on my way because I do not like to condemn anyone to death,' replied the Little Prince.

'No that cannot be,' said the king.

His preparations to leave had been completed but the Little Prince had no intentions of offending the old king so he suggested. 'If your majesty wishes that his commands be promptly obeyed then you should give a reasonable order. You could order me to be gone in a minute. I feel conditions are favourable...'

The king did not respond. Seeing this the Little Prince sighed and took his leave.

As he left, the king called after him in haste, 'I will make you my Ambassador.'

Appreciating the king's air of authority, the Little Prince said to himself. 'The Grown-ups are a strange lot,' and continued on his journey.

A CONCEITED MAN

When he arrived on the second planet, the Little Prince found that it was inhabited by a conceited man.

On seeing the Little Prince at a distance, the man remarked 'Aha! I am being visited by an admirer.'

Truly conceited, because all conceited men see others as their admirers.

'Good Morning,' said the Little Prince.

The conceited man

'That is funny hat you are wearing.'

'This is the hat which I raise in salute when people admire or acclaim me. It is unfortunate that nobody ever passes by,' came the reply.

'Indeed?' was the Little Prince's response because he did not quite understand what the conceited man was talking about.

'Clap your hands,' asked the conceited man.

On hearing this, the Little Prince clapped his hands.

In response the conceited man raised his hat modestly as a salute.

'This is more interesting than my visit to the king on the last planet', said the Little Prince to himself. So he clapped his hands once and the conceited man raised his hat once again.

The Little Prince continued doing so for another five minutes and the conceited man reciprocated by lifting his hat on each occasion. Soon the Little Prince got tired of clapping his hands and asked.

'And what would someone have to do get you to lower your hat.'

The conceited man did not respond to this because conceited men only responded to praises.

Finally the conceited man asked the Little Prince, 'Do you really admire me that much?'

'What does, 'admire' mean?' questioned the Little Prince.'

'It means that you consider me to be the best dressed, handsomest, richest, and the most intelligent person on this planet,' came the prompt reply.

'But there is no one else on this planet,'

said the Little Prince.

'Be kind enough to admire me all the same!'

The Little Prince shrugged his shoulders and said, 'I admire you, but why is it so important for you?'

Saying that the Little Prince walked away.

Continuing his journey, he said to himself, 'Grown-ups are really an odd lot.'

THE DRUNKARD

During a very short visit to the third planet the Little Prince found a Drunkard, sitting silently with a collection of bottles in front of him, some empty and some full.

Though the visit was a short one, it saddened the Little Prince.

On seeing the drunkard the Little Prince asked him, 'What are you doing on this planet?'

A drunkard lived on the third planet

'I am drinking,' said the drunkard.

'But why are you drinking?' asked the Little Prince.

'I am drinking to forget,' responded the drunkard.

Feeling sorry for him the Little Prince continued. 'To forget what?'

'To forget that I am ashamed.'

With a helpful intention the Little Prince asked. 'Ashamed of what?'

'Ashamed of drinking!' said the drunkard before withdrawing into complete silence.

The Little Prince continued with his journey with a firmer belief that the Grown-ups were truly an odd lot.

OWNING THE STARS

Upon arrival the Little Prince found that a businessman inhabited the fourth planet. The businessman was so preoccupied in his work that he did not raise his head from his work upon the Little Prince's arrival.

The Little Prince started the conversation; 'Good Morning!' he said 'your cigarette has gone out.'

'Two and three add up to five, five and seven add up to twelve, twelve and three add up to fifteen. Good Morning! Fifteen and seven add up to twenty-two. Twenty-two and six add up to twenty-eight. I did not find the time to light my cigarette again. Twenty-six and five add up to thirty-one. Phew! All that adds up to five-hundred-and-one million, six-hundred-twenty-two thousand, seven-hundred-thirty-one.'

'Five hundred million of what?' enquired the Little Prince.

'Oh! You are still there, are you? Five-hundred-and-one million... I can't stop... there is so much I have to do! I am engrossed in matters of consequence and I cannot amuse myself with balderdash! Two and five make even...' and the businessman continued.

The Little Prince never let go of a question once he had asked it so he repeated, 'Five-hundred and one-million of what?'

The businessman

On hearing this he businessman raised his head and said.

'I have inhabited his planet for forty-four years and in that duration I have been disturbed only on three occasions. On the first occasion a goose felt giddy and fell down from goodness knows where. He made the most dreadful noises that echoed all over the planet. It was because of him that I made four mistakes in my addition.

Eleven years ago on the second occasion I suffered an attack of rheumatism, from lack of exercise, since I have no time to loaf around and this is the third occasion. As I was saying, five-hundred-and-one million of...'

'Million of what?' persisted the Little Prince.

This time the businessman realised that he

would not be left in peace till he answered the Little Prince's question.

'Millions of those little objects which one sees sometimes in the sky,' said the businessman.

'Flies?' asked the Little Prince.

'Oh! No! The little glittering objects,' replied the businessman.

'Bees?' asked the Little Prince.

'No! No! Small golden objects that lead lazy men into idle dreaming. I have no time for dreaming because of the matters of consequence that I am concerned with.'

'Ah! You mean the stars?' asked the Little Prince.

'Yes! Quite so I was referring to the stars,' came the reply.

'And what is it that you do with the five-million stars?'

'It is Five-hundred-and-one million, six hundred twenty-two thousand, seven hundred thirty-one to be precise, I am accurate since I am handling matter of consequence,' corrected the businessman.

'So what is it that you do with all these stars?' asked the Little Prince.

'What do I do with them?'

'Yes!' said the Little Prince.

'I don't do anything with them, I own them,' replied the businessman.

'You own the stars?'

'Yes.'

'But I have met a king who...'

'Kings never own anything, they rule over them. There is a difference between owning and ruling over something.'

'So what use is it to you to own so many stars?' queried the Little Prince.

'It makes me feel rich,' replied the businessman.

'And what good does it do to feel rich.'

'That is what makes it possible for me to buy more stars, if and when they are discovered.'

The Little Prince said to himself, 'This man reasons quite like the drunkard.'

The Little Prince had some more questions on his mind.

'How can one own the stars?' he asked.

Quite peevishly the businessman asked the Little Prince. 'To whom do they belong?'

'I don't know, to nobody I guess,' replied the Little Prince.

'If they don't belong to anybody, then they belong to me because I was the first one to think about it,' said the businessman.

'Is that reason enough?' continued the Little Prince.' Of course it is reason enough, if you find a diamond that doesn't belong to anybody then don't you keep it. Should you discover an island that does not belong to anyone, isn't it yours for keeps. When you are the first one to get an idea, you take out a patent on it and it is yours. Quite the same I own the stars because nobody thought of owning them before I did.'

'Quite logical,' said the Little Prince. 'But what is it that you do with them.' 'I am the one who manages them, I count them and then recount them,' replied the businessman.' It is matters of consequence that I am concerned with.'

The Little Prince was not satisfied.

'If I owned a silk scarf, I can wrap it around my neck and walk away with it, if I owned a flower, I could pick it and take it away with me. But how can you pick stars?'

'I can't pick them but I can put them in the bank,' said the businessman.' What does that mean?'

'It just means that I write down the number of stars, I have, on a piece of paper, put the paper in a drawer and then lock the drawer with a key.'

'Is that all?' asked the Little Prince. 'It is enough,' replied the businessman

'Quite amusing an poetic,'said the Little Prince, 'but an effort of no real importance.'

The Little Prince's idea of what was important was quite different from what the grown-ups though was important.

'I too own a flower which I water each day,' he said to the businessman. 'Besides the flower I also own three volcanoes which I clean out each week. I always include the one that is extinct. One never knows. The work I do is good for my flower and the volcanoes. But you are of no use to the stars...'

The businessman opened his mouth to say something but he was at a loss of words.

'Grown-ups are beyond comprehension,' said the Little Prince to himself as he continued on his journey.

A THOUSAND SUNSETS

When the Little Prince reached the fifth planet, he found it very strange. It was the smallest of all the planets he had visited so far. In fact it was so small that there was room on it only for a street lamp and a lamplighter. The Little Prince wondered what was purpose a street lamp and a lamplighter would serve on an isolated planet, in the sky, with no houses and no one else living on it.

All the same he said to himself, 'the lamplighter does seem absurd but he is not as absurd as the king, the conceited man, the businessman or the drunkard. At least the lamplighter's work of lighting the lamp has some purpose. At least on lighting the lamp he lights up another star and brings it to life. On extinguishing the lamp he puts the star to sleep. It is a beautiful occupation and since it is beautiful, it is also useful.'

On arriving on the planet, the Little Prince, respectfully, saluted the Lamplighter.

'Good-morning, sir,' said the Little Prince. 'Why have you just put out the lamp?'

'Those are the orders I have,' replied the lamplighter. 'Good-morning!'

'What are the orders you have?'

'The orders I have are that I put out the

Tending to the lamps

lamp. Good-evening.'

Saying that he lit the lamp once again.

The Little Prince was surprised and he asked, 'But why have you just lit the lamp again?'

'Those are the orders,' replied the lamplighter once again.

'I am afraid I don't understand,' said the Little Prince.

'There is not much to understand, orders are orders. Good-morning,' replied the lamplighter.

Having said that the lamplighter put out the lamp

The lamplighter then took out a handkerchief covered with red squares and with it he mopped his brow and said.

'In the good old days my calling was not that terrible, it was reasonable. I use to put the lamp out in the morning and light it in the evening. For the remaining part of the day I would rest and for the remaining part of the night I would sleep.'

'Have the orders been changed since then?' asked the Little Prince.

'No! The tragedy is that the orders have not been changed since then,' replied the lamplighter. As the years have gone by the speed of this planet's rotation has increased but the orders have not been changed.'

'So!' asked the Little Prince.

'Now the planet rotates at the speed of one rotation per minute. And I don't get a second's rest. Now I have to keep lighting and putting out my lamp once every minute,' explained the lamplighter.

'That is funny! You mean to tell me a day lasts only for a minute on your planet?' asked the Little Prince.

'I don't think it is funny, we have already been talking for a month,' replied the lamplighter.

'A whole month?' asked the Little Prince in surprise.

'Yes! Thirty minutes equals to thirty days on this planet. Good-evening.' With that the lamplighter lit his lamp once again.

The Little Prince began to like the lamplighter as he watched him go about his routine. He was very faithful to his orders and he remembered his sunsets, which he used to seek himself by moving his chair on the planet. The Little Prince saw a friend in him and he wanted to help this newfound friend.

'I think I know a way which would allow you to rest whenever you want to...'

'I always want to rest,' interrupted the

lamplighter.

A person can be both, faithful and lazy.

The Little Prince went on: 'your planet is so small that you can walk all around it in barely three strides. If you walk slowly enough you will always stay in the sun. So when you want to rest you begin to walk slowly and the day will last for as long as you like...'

'Walking wouldn't help much,' said the lamplighter. 'The one thing I like in life is sleeping.'

'That is very unfortunate,' said the Little Prince.

'I agree it is indeed unfortunate. Good-morning,' said the lamplighter.

With this he put out his lamp.

As the Little Prince continued on his journey from this planet, he said to himself:

'this man would be despised by all the others, the king, the conceited man the drunkard and by the businessman. But I don't despise him or find him ridiculous. Perhaps it is because he is the only one, I have met so far, who is not only concerned about himself.'

He continued, 'this man is the only one who can be my friend, but this planet is too small for the two of us.'

What the Little Prince could not admit to himself was that he was sorry to leave a planet blessed with one thousand, four hundred and forty sunsets each day.

GEOGRAPHERS AND EXPLORERS

Compared to the fifth planet, the sixth planet was ten times larger it too was inhabited. On this planet there was an old man who was writing thick books.

'Ah, here comes an explorer! He exclaimed to himself on seeing the prince coming.

Having traveled so far, the Little Prince was out of breath so he sat down and panted for a little while.

The old man who wrote in thick books

Seeing him the old gentleman asked: 'Where have you come from?'

Without answering him the Little Prince asked: 'What are you doing and what is that big book?'

· 'I am a geographer,' replied the old man.

'What is a geographer?' asked the Little Prince.

'A scholar who knows the locations of the seas, rivers, mountains, deserts and towns, is called a geographer,' explained the old man.

'That is very interesting, here at last I have found a man who has a real profession!' said the Little Prince. Having said that, the Little Prince looked around and admired the geographer's magnificent and stately planet.

'You have a very beautiful planet,' said the Little Prince. 'Has it any Oceans?'

'I am afraid I can't tell you that,' the geographer replied.

The Little Prince was disappointed. 'Well then, does it have any mountains?' he continued.

'I can't tell you that,' replied the geographer.

Persistently the Little Prince continued, 'and any rivers, towns or deserts.'

'I couldn't tell you that either,' responded the geographer.

'But you said you are a geographer.'

'That is exactly what I said, but I am not an explorer. I don't have a single explorer on my planet. It is not the geographer's job to go and count the rivers, mountains, seas, towns and the deserts. The geographer is much too occupied with his work to perform these trivial tasks. The geographer never leaves his desk. He only receives the explorers in his study. He asks them questions about their travels and makes notes of what they narrate to him. 'If the recollections of the explorers are found interesting then the geographer orders an enquiry into his moral character.'

'But why do you do that?' asked the Little Prince.

'It is done because if an explorer is telling lies then he will bring a bad name to the geographer's books. Quite like an explorer who drinks too much,' replied the geographer.

' But why?' persisted the Little Prince.

'Simply because drunkards see double and a drunk explorer would narrate two mountains where in reality he sees one,' elaborated the geographer.

'I understand because I know someone who would make a bad explorer.'

'Quite possible,' replied the geographer. 'Even if the moral character of an explorer is found satisfactory, I order an enquiry into his discovery.'

'You mean someone goes to check it?' asked the Little Prince.

'No. That would be too complicated to do. Instead we ask the explorer to furnish proof of his discovery. If, as an example, he has discovered a large mountain, then he is required to bring back some large stones from it to prove his discovery.' Quite suddenly the geographer got excited and said: 'you too have come a long way! You too are an explorer! Can you describe your planet to me?'

Having said this the Geographer having

sharpened his pencil opened his register. 'One starts off by noting the explorer's story in pencil and once the explorer has provided the required proof, the noting is inked.'

'Well! What do you have to say?' the geographer asked expectantly.

'Oh! You are referring to where I live,' said the Little Prince. 'My planet is not very interesting. It is very small. I have three volcanoes, two of which are active while the third is extinct, But you never know.'

'I agree, one never knows,' agreed the geographer.

'Oh! I also have a flower,' the Little Prince recollected.

'I am afraid we don't record flowers,' said the geographer.

'Why not? Is it actually the prettiest thing on my planet.'

'It is because flowers are ephemeral,' explained the geographer.

'And what does "ephemeral" mean?'

'Geographies are the most precious of all books,' said the geographer. 'They never go out of fashion. You see a mountain does not change its position, neither does an ocean empty out all its water. Hence we record eternal things.'

'Extinct volcanoes can of course wake up,' interrupted the Little Prince. 'What does ephemeral mean?' asked the Little Prince, not willing to let go of his question.

'It means 'in danger of disappearing quickly.' Explained the geographer.

'Of course it does.'

'So my flower is ephemeral,' said the Little Prince to himself, 'and she has but four thorns to defend herself from the world!

Oh my! I have left her alone on my planet.

Though in regret, the Little Prince mustered up his courage and asked: 'Which place would you advise me to visit next?'

'Visit the Planet earth, it has a good reputation...'

With that the Little Prince left. Thoughts of his little flower still on his mind.

"Which place should I visit next?"

EARTH AN EXTRAORDINARY PLANET

This is how the Little Prince came to Earth, the seventh planet in his journey.

Earth was no ordinary planet!

On the earth there were 111 kings (including the Negro kings among them), there were 7,000 geographers, 900,000 businessmen, 7,500,000 drunkards, 311,000,000-conceited man. In other words there were around 2,000,000,000 grown-ups'

You can get an idea of the size of earth when I tell you that, before the discovery of electricity, it was necessary to maintain a force of 462,511 men as lamplighters to light the street lamps in the six continents.

When seen from a distance, it was quite a spectacle, to see the movement of this army of lamplighters. It was quite like the movements of the artistes in a ballet.

To start with, the lamplighters of New Zealand and Australia would appear and light the street lamps, having done this they would go off to sleep. Following them, the lamplighters of India, China and Siberia would make their appearance for there steps in the ballet. Once their job was done, they too would retreat into the wings.

Next came the lamplighters of Russia and the Indies; followed by the lamplighters of South America and finally North America.

The entire performance was smooth and no one made a mistake in the order of appearance on the stage. It was a magnificent performance to watch.

The only two lamplighters who led a toil and care free life were the lamplighters at the North Pole and the one at the South Pole. Each of these men had a single lamp to light to take care of and they had to so only twice in a whole year.

THE SNAKE

When one wishes to be witty, one may wander a little from the truth. For that matter I have not been completely truthful while narrating to you about the lamplighters.

This is why I run the risk of giving you a false impression, about earth, to those who do not know about it. Humans occupy only a small part of the earth.

If we were to get all, two billion of them, to stand upright in a small area, quite like in a public assembly, they would all fit into a square twenty miles long and twenty miles wide. All humans would fit into an area the size of a small Pacific Islet.

I am sure the grown-ups would not believe you if you told them that. They think they occupy a lot of space.

They consider themselves to be as important as the baobabs. It is best, then, to advise them to calculate on their own. Since they are fond of figures, you will please them by asking them to do so.

However don't waste your time by doing this. It is unnecessary for I know you have confidence in me.

When the Little Prince arrived on the earth, he was surprised at not finding anyone. Initially he thought, he had come to the wrong planet, until a coil of gold, quite like the colour of moonlight flashed across the sand in front of him.

Seeing it the Little Prince courteously said: 'Good Evening!'

'Good evening,' responded the snake.

'Which planet am I on now?' asked the Little Prince.

'This is Africa, on the planet earth,' replied the snake.

'Ah? Are there no people on earth?'

'The earth is very large and this is a desert. There are no people in the desert,' said the snake.

Hearing this the Little Prince sat down on a stone and raised his head to look at the sky.

'I wonder if the stars are lit up in the sky each day so that we have no difficulty in finding our own some day... Look there is my planet, it is right above us. But it is far away!' said the Little Prince.

'It is beautiful. But what has brought you so far away?' asked the snake.

'I have been troubled because of a flower,' replied the Little Prince.

'Ah!' responded the snake.

With that they both fell silent.

Picking up a conversation once again the Little Prince asked: 'Where are all the people, is it not lonely in the desert?'

'One can be lonely even when one is amongst people,' replied the snake.

The Little Prince gazed at the snake, silently for some time.

'You are a strange animal,' he said finally. 'You are no thicker than a finger.'

Talking to the snake

'So be it, but I am more powerful than a king's finger,' replied the snake.

Hearing this the Little Prince smiled.

'I don't think you are powerful; you don't even have any feet. You cannot travel....'

'So what! I can carry you farther than any ship,' interrupted the snake.

With this the snake wrapped himself around the Little Prince's ankle, quite like a bracelet of gold.

'Whomsoever I touch, I return to the earth from whence they came, but you are innocent and you come from a star...' said the snake.

The Little Prince remained silent.

'I pity you, you are weak on earth which is made of granite,' continued the snake. 'Maybe someday I can help you, should you grow homesick for your planet. I can...'

'I understand what you say, but tell me,

why do you always speak in riddles,' said the Little Prince.

'It is so because I solve them all.'

Once again they both fell silent.

A LONE FLOWER

The Little Prince moved on and crossed the desert. It was here that he met a lone flower. The flower had four petals.

'Good morning!' the Little Prince greeted the flower.

'Good morning,' responded the flower.

'Where are all the men?' asked the Little Prince politely.

Finding the little flower

Quite some time back the flower had seen a caravan passing by.

'Men?' questioned the flower. 'I know that there are six or seven men in existence because I saw them several years ago. But I do not know how to find them now. Since they have no roots, the wind blows them away and this makes their life very difficult,' explained the flower.

Hearing this the Little Prince bid the flower farewell and moved on.

ON TOP OF A MOUNTAIN

The Little Prince saw a high mountain and climbed it. He had not seen such a high mountain. He knew only of his three volcanoes, which were as high as his knees and one of which, the extinct one, served him as a footstool.

'Once on the top of a mountain as high as this one,' he said to himself, 'I will be able to see the whole planet and all the people on it...'

Unfortunately he saw nothing but the sharp, needle like, peaks of rock.

'Good morning,' he said out of courtesy.

'Good morning... Good morning... Good morning...' came the echo all around him.

'Who are you?' asked the Little Prince.

'Who are you... Who are you... Who are you?' repeated the echo.

'Become my friend. I am all alone.' said the Little Prince.

'I am all alone... all alone... all alone...' came the echo.

'What a strange planet,' thought the Little Prince in surprise.

'This planet is dry, pointed, harsh and forbidding. The people are not imaginative and they repeat whatever you say to them. On my planet I had a flower and she was always the first to speak...'

On top of the mountain

THE GARDEN OF ROSES

The Little Prince walked for quite some time over sand, rock and snow. Finally he came upon a road. He knew that all roads led the homes of men.

Standing before a garden full of roses in full bloom the Little Prince said: 'Good Morning.'

'Good Morning,' responded the roses.

The Little Prince stared at them in

‘Who are you?’ he asked in awe.

surprise, they all looked like his flower.

'Who are you?' he asked in awe.

'We are roses,' replied the flowers.

The response saddened him because his flower had told him that she was the only one in the universe. But here he saw five thousand flowers like her, all alike, and that too in a single garden!

'She would be very annoyed if she could see so many flowers like her. For sure, she would cough dreadfully and pretend she was dying, just to avoid being laughed at. Then I would have to pretend that I was nursing her back to life. I know, if I did not do that to show that I was humble, she would surely die...'

Continuing to reflect: 'I thought I was rich because I possessed a flower that was unique, only to find that all I had was a common rose... a common rose and three volcanoes as high as my knees, with one of them, which may remain extinct forever.'

With just all that I am not really a great prince. With these thoughts in mind the Little Prince lay down on the grass and cried.

TAMING THE FOX

The Little Prince did not see a fox appear.

'Good morning,' said the fox to the Little Prince.

'Good morning,' the Little Prince responded as he turned around but he could not see who had wished him.

'I am right here, under the apple tree,' came the voice.

'Who might you be?' asked the Little Prince and continued: 'you are very pretty to look at.'

'I am a fox,' came the response.

'I am unhappy. Would you like to play with me?' asked the Little Prince.

'I am afraid I cannot play with you, I am not tamed,' replied the fox.

'Oh! Please excuse me, I did not know that,' said the Little Prince.

After some thought the Little Prince asked: What does tame mean?'

'Apparently you are not from here,' said the fox. What are you looking for?'

'I am looking for men, but what do you mean by "tame"?'

'Men have guns and they hunt. It is very disturbing. They also like to raise chickens.

“Are you looking for chickens?”

They have only two interests, hunting and raising chickens,' said the fox. 'Are you looking for chickens?'

'No I am not looking for chickens, I am looking for friends. What do you mean by tame?'

'Tame means establishing ties, and it something that is often neglected.'

'Establish ties?' questioned the Little Prince.

'Precisely,' replied the fox. 'As far as I am concerned you are just a little boy, quite like a hundred thousand other boys. I have no need for you and likewise you have no need or me. To you, I too, am just another fox quite like a hundred thousand other foxes. Should you tame me then we will need each other. It is then that we will become unique to each other.'

'I understand what you are trying to tell me,' said the Little Prince. 'There is a little flower... I think she has tamed me...'

'It is quite possible, there are all sorts of things you can see on earth.'

'Oh! But it is not a flower on earth that I am talking about,' said the Little Prince.

The fox was a little confused but out of curiosity he asked: 'If not on earth then on another planet?'

'Yes,' replied the Little Prince.

'Are there hunters on that planet?'

'No!'

'Nothing is perfect,' said the fox with a sigh.

'I lead a monotonous life,' he continued. 'I

The hunter

hunt chickens and the men hunt me, we are all alike. As a result I feel bored. But should you tame me, it will be like a new day had dawned and the sun had begun to shine in my life. I will finally know the sounds of your footsteps, which will be different from all the others. While the sound of other footsteps sends me scurrying for shelter, the sound of your footsteps will be like music to my ears, which will beckon me out of my burrow.'

The fox continued: 'do you see the fields of wheat in the distance? They are of no use to me because I do not eat bread. That is why the wheat fields don't have anything to say to me. It makes me sad. You have golden hair quite like the golden fields of wheat. Once you have tamed me, the wheat will remind me of your hair and I will love to listen to the wind as it blows over the wheat fields...'

The fox fell silent and gazed at the Little Prince for some time. Finally he pleaded: 'Please tame me.'

'Much that I want to do so, I am afraid I can't, I have to move on and discover new friends and understand many new things,' replied the Little Prince.

'You can understand only what you tame,' said the fox. 'Men do not have the time to understand anything. They like to buy everything readymade from the shops, but where does one buy friendship. Since there are no shops selling friendship, men do not have any friends any more. So if you want a friend, tame me...'

'What is it that I have to do to tame you,' asked the Little Prince.

'To tame me you will have to be patient,'

replied the fox. To start with, you have sit at a distance from me on the grass. I shall look at you but you will not say anything. You see! Words can create misunderstandings. With the passing of each day, you will sit closer and closer to me...'

The next morning, the Little Prince came back. 'It would have been better if you had come at the same time as yesterday,' said the fox. 'For example, knowing that you would be coming at four o'clock in the afternoon, I would have begun to feel good at three o'clock. And as the hour would have advanced my eagerness would increase and by four o'clock I would be jumping about, waiting for you. But if you come at any time, unannounced, my heart would not be ready to greet you. It is necessary that we observe the proper rites...'

'What do you mean by "rite"?' questioned the Little Prince.

'Rites are actions which are often neglected,' replied the fox.

'Rites make one day different from the other,' continued the fox. 'Even hunters have rites; on every Thursday they dance with the girls in the village. That is why Thursdays are wonderful for me, on that day I can walk around in the vineyards without any fear of being hunted. However, if the hunters danced on all days of the week, then every day would be like the other and I would not have a holiday at all.'

It was then, that the Little Prince tamed the fox.

When the time came for the Little Prince to leave: 'Oh!' said the fox, 'I will cry.'

'If you do so it will be your own fault, I have

done nothing to harm you, it is you who wanted to be tamed.'

'I agree with that,' replied the fox.

'And then you want to cry!' said the Little Prince.

'Yes, I want to cry,' replied the fox.

'You mean to say, it has done you no good at all.'

'On the contrary, it has done me good,' said the fox. Because of the colour of the wheat fields...' And then he continued:

'Go back to the roses and look at the again, it is now that you will understand that your flower is unique in all the planets. Once you have done so come back to me and I will tell you a secret.'

As asked by the fox, the Little Prince went to see the roses for a second time.

'You are not at all like my rose, till now you

are nothing. No one has tamed you and you have tamed no one. You are quite like my fox when I met him for the first time. At that time he was just another fox amongst a hundred thousand other foxes. But now he is unique because I have tamed him and he is now my friend.'

The Little Prince's words embarrassed the roses.

'You are beautiful but no one would die for you. It is quite possible that an ordinary passer-by may think that you look like my rose. But I know that she is the most important rose amongst hundreds of thousands of roses like you. It is so because it is her that I have sheltered behind a screen. It was for her that I killed all the caterpillars, all except the two or three we saved so that they would become butterflies. It is her that I have listened to whenever she boasted or grumbled, all because she is my rose.'

Having said that, the Little Prince went back to the fox.

'Good day,' he said to the fox when he arrived.

'Good day,' responded the fox. 'As promised I will now tell you a simple secret.'

'It is only with the heart that you see what is right, for what is essential is invisible to the eye,' said the fox.

'What is essential is invisible to the eye,' repeated the Little Prince after the fox so that he would not forget what the fox had said.

'Remember, it is the time you have spent with the rose that makes it so special and important for you,' added the fox.

'The time I have spent with my rose...'

A responsibility to the roses

repeated the Little Prince so that he would remember the fox's words.

'Most people have forgotten this truth, but you must remember it. Once you have tamed something, you become responsible for it forever. Similarly you are responsible for your rose,' said the fox.

'I am responsible for the rose,' repeated the Little Prince, confining the words to his memory.

SORTING THE TRAVELERS

As he walked on the Little Prince met a railway switchman.

'Good morning,' he said to him.

'Good Morning,' replied the railway switchman.

'What is it that you do here,' the Little Prince asked him.

'I sort out the travelers in bundles of

thousands and send off the trains that carry them. Some to the right and some to the left,' replied the railway switchman.

Just then a brightly lit express train shook the railway switchman's cabin as it thundered by.'They seem to be in a great hurry. What is it they are looking for?' asked the Little Prince.

'I am afraid not even the locomotive's engineer is aware of that,' replied the railway switchman.

Just then another brilliantly lit express train thundered by from the opposite direction.

'Are they coming back so soon?' asked the Little Prince.

This is not the same train, it is an exchange,' came the reply.

'Why is it so, were they not satisfied with

where they were?'

'No one is ever satisfied with where they are,' said the railway switchman.

With that the cabin shook again as a third express train roared by.

'Are the travelers in this train pursuing the travelers in the first train?' queried the Little Prince.

'They are not pursuing anything; they are all asleep in the train and if they are not asleep than they must be yawning. It is only the children who are awake and flattening their noses against the windowpanes,' replied the railway switchman.

'Is it only the children who know what they are looking for? Usually they waste their time over rag dolls which are very important for them and if anyone takes it away from them then they cry.'

'They are lucky,' replied the switchman.

With that the Little Prince moved on.

SAVING TIME

Next the Little Prince met a merchant.

'Good morning,' the Little Prince greeted him.

'Good morning,' came the reply.

This merchant sold little pills that had been invented to quench thirst. All you had to do was, swallow a single pill once a week and you would not feel the urge to drink anything.

'Why are you selling these pills?' asked the Little Prince.'

'I sell them because they save a lot of time,' replied the merchant. 'Experts have made computations that prove that by consuming these pills you save fifty-three minutes in a week.'

'So what do you do with the fifty-three minutes you have saved,' asked the Little Prince.

'Anything you would like to...'

'If I had these fifty-three minutes to spend, I would leisurely walk towards a spring of fresh water,' said the Little Prince to himself.

IN SEARCH OF WATER

Eight days had passed since I had the accident in the desert with my plane. I heard the story of the merchant as I drank the last drop of the water I had with me.

'These memories that you have narrated to me are interesting. I am afraid I have not succeeded in repairing my plane and I have no more water to drink. I too would be happy to walk leisurely with you to the spring of water.'

'My friend the fox...' began the Little Prince.

'My friend the matter at hand has nothing to do with the fox,' I interrupted.

'Why Not?' came the response.

'Simply because I am about to die of thirst...'

Without following my reasoning he responded:

'Even if you are about to die, it is always good to have a friend. For that matter I am glad I have the fox as a friend' said the Little Prince.'

'There is no way by which he can understand the gravity of the situation I am in,' I said to myself. He has never gone thirsty or hungry. All he needs is a little sunshine.'

As if understanding my thoughts, he gave me a steady look and said: 'I too am thirsty, lets look for a spring.'

I responded to his absurd suggestion with a gesture of weariness because it is absurd to go looking for a spring at random in such a large desert. Nevertheless we started walking.

We trudged along for several hours in silence. Soon the sun set, it became dark, and the stars came out. By then my thirst had made me a little feverish. I looked at the stars as if I was in a dream. I recollected the Little Prince's last words and asked him:

'So you too are thirsty?'

He did not respond to my question, instead he said:

'Water is also good for the heart...'

Though I did not understand the answer, said nothing. I knew better than to question him. Something that was impossible to do.

I could see that he was tired so he sat down.

I did the same since I too was tired.

We sat in silence for a few moments then he spoke again:

'The stars look beautiful only because there is a flower that cannot be seen by us.'

'Yes I agree!' I replied. Saying that I looked across the dunes of sand in the desert that stretched before us in the moonlight.

'The desert too is beautiful,' added the Little Prince.

It was true and I agreed with him. I had always loved the desert; you could sit on a sand dune and watch the desert without seeing anything in particular or without hearing a sound. Yet the desert throbbed and gleamed...'

'What do you think makes the desert so beautiful?' asked the Little Prince and continued: 'Is it because somewhere in its expanse it hides a well...'

The Little Prince's words astonished me. I suddenly understood the mystery of the sands. I recalled that as a little boy I lived in an old house and legends told us that there was a treasure buried in that house. No one had known how to find it and no one had found it either. Probably because no one had, actually, tried to look for it. But all this gave the house an enchanted feel, simply because it housed a treasure somewhere in its heart...

'Yes I agree,' I said to the Little Prince. 'The stars, the desert and the house are beautiful because they have within them something that is invisible!'

'I am glad that you agree with my fox,' said

the Little Prince.

Having said that the Little Prince dropped off to sleep so I took him in my arms and began walking once again. I felt deeply moved and my soul felt stirred. It was as if I was carrying the most precious and fragile treasure on earth.

In the moonlight I looked at his pale forehead, closed eyes and his locks of hair that trembled in the wind and said to myself: 'What I see here is but a shell. What is important is invisible...'

In his slumber the Little Prince's lips opened slightly in half a smile. I looked at him and said to myself, yet again: 'I am moved by the Little Prince's loyalty to a flower and the image of the rose shines through him like the flame of a lamp, even when he sleeps.' I felt him becoming more fragile and I wanted to protect him. Afraid that, as if, he were a small flame that may be extinguished by a puff of wind...

With that I walked on till I found a well of water at daybreak.

QUENCHING THEIR THIRST

'Men set out on their way in express trains without knowing what they are looking for. Then they run around in excitement...' said the Little Prince.

Continuing he added: 'It is not worth the trouble...'

The well of water that we had discovered was different from the other wells in the Sahara. The other wells were merely holes

Finding a well at daybreak

that had been dug in the sand. This one was very much like a well you would see in a village. Yet there was no village around, which led me to believe that I was dreaming.

'Very strange.' I said to the Little Prince. 'There is everything you need, a pulley, a bucket, some rope...'

The Little Prince laughed and touched the rope. The pulley was set in motion, it squeaked and made a moaning sound, quite like an old weathervane makes when the wind blows.

'We seem to have wakened the well, you can hear it singing,' said the Little Prince on hearing the sound.

I knew the Little Prince was exhausted after the journey so I said to him: 'Let me handle it, it is too heavy for you.'

Slowly I hoisted the bucket of water to the

top of the well and set it on the edge of the well. With the sounds of the pulley still in my ears I rested on my laurels and looked at the reflection of the sun in the bucket of water.

'I am very thirsty, give me some water to drink,' said the Little Prince.

I understood what the Little Prince was looking for so I raised the bucket to his lips and he drank the water. His eyes were closed as if he was savouring some sweet festive treat instead of ordinary water. The water seemed to have been sweetened by our walk under the stars, the sound of the pulley and the effort of my arms.

'Where you live, do the men raise five thousand roses in the same garden and still don't find in it what they are looking for,' the Little Prince asked me after quenching his thirst.

'They do not find it,' I replied in agreement.

'Surprisingly, what they are looking for can well be found in a single rose or in very little water.' Said the Little Prince.

'Yes that is quite true,' I replied.

Hearing this the Little Prince added:

'Surely they would know that in such matters the eyes are blind, you must look with your heart...'

Having drunk a little water, I breathed more easily. In the morning the desert sand has the same colour, as honey and this made me feel happy. Why then did I have within me a sense of grief?

The Little Prince came and sat next to me and said very softly: 'You must keep your promise.'

'What promise?' I asked him.

'You remember... a muzzle for my sheep, I am responsible for the flower...'

I dug into my pocket and pulled out my drawings. Seeing them the Little Prince laughed and said:

'Your baobabs... they look quite like cabbages.'

'Oh! Do they?' I asked. I hade been quite proud of the baobabs I had drawn.

'Your fox... his ears look like horns, they are too long,' he continued.

Having said that he laughed again.

'That is not fair Little Prince,' I replied. 'I only know how to draw boa constrictors from the inside and from the outside.'

'Oh! That is all right, children understand,' he replied.

I took out my pencil and sketched a muzzle for the sheep and gave it to him.

'I think you have plans that I am not aware of,' I said to him.

Instead of answering me he said:

'You know... my arrival on earth... tomorrow will be its anniversary.

After a moment of silence he continued: 'I arrived very close to this place.'

With that he flushed a little.

The feeling of grief was still there within me, I failed to understand why. There was of course one thought in my mind so I asked:

'So it was not a matter of chance that I met you, a week ago, strolling along thousands of miles from any habitation? You were merely on your way back to the place where you had landed?'

Hearing this the Little Prince flushed once again.

Hesitating a little I added:

'Probably it was because of the anniversary.'

The Little Prince flushed a little more. He never answered the questions but can't one take a flush to be an answer in the affirmative.

'Ah, I think I am a little frightened...'

Here he interrupted me.

'Now you must return to your plane and repair the engine. I will wait for you here. You can come back tomorrow evening.'

Something bothered me I was not reassured. I remembered what the fox had said. You run the risk of weeping a little if you let yourself be tamed.

GOING BACK HOME

Next to the well there was the ruin of an old stone wall. On my return, from the plane, the next evening, from a distance I saw the Little Prince sitting on top of the stone wall with his feet dangling over the side. I heard him say:

'It is obvious you don't remember. This is not the exact spot.'

He must have been conversing with some

one who had answered him because he then continued:

Yes! It is indeed the correct day but this is not the same place.'

As I came close I failed to see anyone else near him. The Little Prince however continued:

'Exactly! You can find the spot where my tracks begin in the sand and you can wait for me there. I will meet you there tonight.'

I was about twenty yards from the wall but I still failed to see anyone besides the Little Prince.

After a moment's silence the Little Prince spoke again. 'Your poison is good? You are sure it will not make me suffer for too long?'

Hearing that I almost stopped in my tracks and my heart felt torn. The Little Prince continued: 'Now go away, I want to get down from this wall.'

A yellow snake sat below the rock

I looked at the base of the wall and was startled. At the foot of the wall and facing the Little Prince was one of those yellow snakes, which can end your life with a bite, within thirty seconds. I stepped back as I dug into my pocket to pull out my revolver, the noise warned the snake of my presence and it disappeared amongst the stones.

I just made it to the wall in time to catch the Little Prince in my arms, his face was white as snow.

'What is the meaning of this? Why were you talking to the snake?' I asked him.

While I asked him that I loosened the yellow scarf he wore, moistened his temples and given him some water to drink.

He looked at me with a grave expression on his face and put his arms around my neck. His heartbeat felt like that of a dying bird, which had been shot with a rifle.

'How do you know about that?' he said in a weak tone.

I had come over to tell him that the repairs of the plane had been successful.

He made no attempt to answer my question, instead added:

'I, too, am going back to my home today...'

In a sad tone he continued:

'It is much farther... It will be much more difficult...'

It was then that I realised that something very extraordinary was happening. Though I was holding him close to myself, in my arms, quite like a child, he seemed to be slipping headlong into an abyss from which I could not hold him back...

He had a serious expression on his face and a distant look in his eyes.

'I have your sheep, the sheep's box and the muzzle you gave me...' said the Little Prince.

Having said that he gave me a sad smile.

I waited for a long time because I saw him reviving a little.

'My dear little man,' I said to him, 'You are afraid...'

I knew he was afraid but he laughed it off.

'Not yet, I will be much more scared this evening...'

I felt myself in a situation that seemed irreparable. I could not bear the thought of not being able to hear his laughter every now and then. For me it had been like a spring of fresh water in the desert.

'My little man, I want to hear your laughter once again.'

Instead he said to me:

'Tonight it will be a year from the day on which I came to the earth. Tonight my star will be right above the place where I landed a year ago.'

'Little Prince tell me that this is but a bad dream. The snake, the meeting place, the star…'

He did not answer. Instead he said:

'The thing that is important cannot be seen…'

'Yes I know that…'

'It is quite the same, as with the flower. If you love a flower on a star then you will like to look at the sky because all the stars will be a-bloom with flowers…'

'Yes I know that…'

'It is just as it is with water. Because of the pulley and the rope the water you gave me to drink seemed sweet. You remember how good it was.'

'Yes I know that.'

'My star is so small that I cannot show it to you in the sky. It is best that my star remains as one of the stars in the sky. At night, you will like to look up at the stars because amongst them there is one star that is my home you will like to watch all the stars in the heavens. This way all the stars in the sky will be our friends. I would now like to give you a present.'

Having said that he laughed again.

'My dear Little Prince, I love to hear the sound of your laughter! That is a gift enough. Just that is enough.

'Everyone has stars,' he continued, 'but they have different meanings for different people. The travelers see them as guides, for others they are no more than lights in the sky. For scholars, they are problems. For my businessman they were wealth. All such stars are silent. You... You alone...'

'What is it that you are trying to say?'

'I shall be living in one of the stars. I shall be laughing in one of them. That is why it will seem to you that al the stars are alive and all of them are laughing, when you look up into the sky at night... Only you will have stars that can laugh.'

With that he laughed once again.

'Time soothes all sorrows and when your sorrow is comforted, you will be content with the thought that you have known me. You will always be my friend. You will open your window for the pleasure of laughing with me. Your friends will probably be astonished to see you laughing at the night sky. It is then that you will tell them, 'Yes the stars always make me laugh!' They will think you are crazy. It is quite a shabby trick I would have played upon you...'

He laughed once again.

'It will seem as if, in place of stars, I have given you a large number of small bells that know how to laugh...'

Having laughed once again, he became serious and said:

'Don't come tonight...' he said.

'I am afraid I cannot leave you,' I replied.

'I will look like someone who is suffering and dying. It is like that, but do not come to see it. It is not worth the trouble...'

'No! I shall not leave you,' I replied firmly.

He seemed worried.

The Little Prince asked him to go away

'I am also stopping you from coming, because of the snake. Snakes are malicious creatures; he might bite you just for fun...'

'I shall not leave you.'

He relaxed a little as if a reassuring thought came to his mind and he said:

' Is it true that snakes have no poison left in them for a second bite.'

That night I did not see the Little Prince set out on his journey. He left quietly without making a sound. When I caught up with him he was walking along quickly with resolve on his mind. On seeing me he said:

'Ah! There you are...'

Though he seemed worried. He took my hand.

'You should not have come. You will suffer as a consequence. Though I will look as if I have died, it will not be true...'

I was quiet.

'You must understand... I have to go very far and I cannot carry this body with me, it is too heavy.'

I still said nothing.

'The body will be like an old abandoned shell and you don't have to feel sad about old shells...'

I had nothing to say.

Though he was slightly discouraged, he made one more effort and said:

'I too will look at all the stars, for me all the stars will be wells with rusty pulleys and all the stars will pour out fresh and sweet water for me to drink...'

I remained silent.

'It will be very amusing, you will have five hundred million little bells while I will have five million little springs of fresh and sweet water...'

'He could say no more because he had tears in his eyes.'

' From here on let me go on by myself.'

Having said that he sat down because he was afraid. Then again he said:

'You remember my flower... I am responsible for her... She is weak and she is naïve. She has four thorns, which are of no use, to protect herself from the world...'

I was not able to stand any longer so I sat down next to him.

' That is al I have to say.'

A little hesitantly he got up and took a step.

Lost in his thoughts

The sand cushioned his fall

All I could see was a flash of yellow close to his ankle. He was motionless for an instant. Without a cry he fell as gently as a tree falls. There was not a sound as the sand cushioned his fall.

WAITING UNDER THE STARS

Six years have gone by... I have never narrated this story. My friends, who met me on my return, were content on seeing me alive. I did not disclose to them that I was sad at heart. I just told them: 'I am tired.'

I now feel a little comforted because I know he went back to his planet, for I did not find his body in the morning. It was not such a heavy body after all. At night I love to listen to the stars. They sound like five hundred million little bells...

There was one thing that bothered me. When I drew the muzzle for the Little Prince's sheep. I forgot to draw a strap on it. I don't know how the Little Prince will fasten it on the Sheep's mouth. I keep wondering what will happen to the flower on his planet. Will the sheep eat the flower he loves?

Then again I recall the Little Prince covers his flower with a glass globe every night and he also watches over his sheep. There is consolation enough in the laughter of the stars.

On occasions I say to myself:

'It is quite possible that the Little Prince forgets to cover the flower with the glass globe or if the sheep slips out at night without making any noise. What then?'

For all of us who love the Little Prince, the question will remain unanswered and nothing will ever be the same again in the universe till we don't find out if a sheep, we never saw, has eaten or not eaten a rose...

Each night look up at the sky and ask yourself: Has the sheep eaten the flower or not? It is then that you will see how everything changes...

Yet no grown-up will ever understand that this is a matter of great importance.

This is, to me, the saddest and loveliest landscape in the world. It is the same as I had drawn earlier, but I have drawn it again so that you can remember that it is here that the Little Prince appeared on the earth and then disappeared.

See it carefully so that you can recall it, should you travel to the African desert some day. If you happen to come upon this spot do not hurry along. Wait for some time under the star. If a little man, with golden hair, who laughs a lot and refuses to answer questions, appears you will know who he is. If this should ever happen, please comfort me, let me know that he has come back.